MW01294383

The Honest Guide to Successful Pier and Coastal Fishing

The Book for the Uninformed, First Timer, and
Anyone who Wants to Catch More Fish

BRIAN PERRY

WESTBOW
PRESS
A DIVISION OF THOMAS NELSON

WestBow Press books may be ordered through booksellers or by contacting:

WestBow Press
A Division of Thomas Nelson
1663 Liberty Drive
Bloomington, IN 47403
www.westbowpress.com
1-(866) 928-1240

ISBN: 978-1-4497-3659-0 (sc)
ISBN: 978-1-4497-3660-6 (e)

Library of Congress Control Number: 2012900471

Printed in the United States of America

WestBow Press rev. date: 01/23/2012

Preface

My Dad and I have fished together for nearly every year of my life and have been blessed with memories that will last a lifetime. Whether we caught fish or not the fellowship and camaraderie allowed us to make the most out of every trip. True fishermen enjoy the pursuit of the fish perhaps more than the actual catch. Spending a beautiful summer day with good company, while smelling the fresh air right off of the water, will do wonders for the soul and for your health, both mental and physical.

With this book my intent is to show people some very basic and some not so basic techniques to catch fish, with the hope that increased catches will motivate folks to stay with the wonderful tradition of recreational fishing. Again, the pursuit of the fish can make up some of the most rewarding times you will have, but actually landing what you are aiming for can certainly put a smile on the surliest fisherman's face! Let us also not forget that coming home empty handed too many times might make our significant other a little more apprehensive about us buying the newest, most expensive fishing gear that we just had to have. So, let's look at things this way . . . . this book could just give you that extra leverage to keep the wife or husband from giving you the 'ol "you never catch anything!" speech that I am sure most of us have heard more than once!

Tight lines and hang on for some 'average Joe' tips that might just get your rod bent like never before!

Foreword

Saltwater

Saltwater fishing is often times thought of as "too hard", "only for commercial guys in big boats", "only done on charter boats", "standing on a pier in the sun catching nothing" or "too expensive for me to have saltwater and freshwater tackle".

All of those comments and many more can absolutely be true, and often if you don't live near the coast those instances are the only ones you can relate to because that is what you have seen on vacation or television. However, I am going to give you some tips and the actual baits, lures and tackle recommendations to use so you can go out there and fish productively right next to a local. And let me tell you, those old guys on the piers may just look like they are standing there in the sun but they are catching fish and they are learning technique. However, don't be surprised that they don't run up to you and coach you along on how to catch fish. Unfortunately, novice fisherman can cause a lot of trouble on piers, waterways etc . . . Some people just lack common sense and some are just missing out on proper etiquette to be used when fishing around locals or professionals. We will touch on etiquette that can help keep you from standing all by yourself when you are fishing around others.

Chapter 1

Etiquette on piers

1) Fish only as many poles as you can manage, do not have lines strung out everywhere where they can entangle other peoples lines.

2) Throw away your trash and any other trash you may see left unattended. This will go a long way toward making you look like a conscientious fisherman/woman.

3) Smile or nod to the folks around you, especially the old guys. Don't forget a lot of these fellows charged the beach on D-day, secured airfields in the Pacific, perhaps landed at Inchon or faced the horrors in Vietnam. As your parents told you as a child, respect your elders. You never know who you might be fishing with on a given day. Some of the most interesting people I have ever met have been on a pier. Just like the double amputee, Afghanistan war veteran that I spoke with who walks over 1000' foot on 2 artificial legs to make it to his favorite spot on a pier, on a daily basis. Enjoy your time with some great folks from all walks of life.

4) Share your bait when you leave. It makes a great impression, especially if you will be coming back to fish again, if the folks see you offer your remaining bait to those who remain on the pier to fish.

5) Don't take offense if some folks don't warm up to you right away. Remember they come from all walks of life and some are truly there as a form of therapy and are fighting internal battles that you or I may not be aware of. Just maintain your good composure and enjoy yourself and show them you know how to fish and start bringing in your catch!

Chapter 2

Saltwater fishing 101

You can catch fish with whatever kind of equipment (rod and reel) you already have but just make sure you are targeting only the fish that your equipment can handle. Everybody winds up hooking something huge every once in awhile while fishing for small fish and gets their line broke, which is fine. But, it is the joker who keeps fishing for 20 lb. Red Drum with a $20 lightweight Wal-mart rod that will tick people off as they see you tangle everyone who is nearby in your line as the fish makes a run before snapping off. So, fish smart and be productive where you can.

The right tackle/gear

A normal light or light/medium spin cast rod with an average spin cast reel. (Literally a $20 Wal-Mart combo or Dick's combo) will serve you just fine for many species on a pier up to about 3 lbs. You will be able to land these fish effectively with just the rod and reel and pulling the fish up. Fish such as Croaker, Spot, Whiting, Speckled Sea Trout, Grey Trout, Pompano, Small Jacks, Small Flounder, Small Sheepshead, Small Bluefish and Spanish Mackerel are all very common fish that you can catch with this most basic equipment and each are some of your most tasty fish if you choose to keep them for a few meals.

Medium or medium/heavy spin cast combos with, again, an average spin cast reel will do you perfectly for both the above listed smaller fish and those most sought after 3 lb. to 20 lb. lunkers. Fish such as: Red Drum, Black Drum, Doormat Flounder, Large Sheepshead, Stripers, Small Cobia, Chopper Blue Fish, Large Spanish Mackerel, and big Jack fish. These rods should be spooled with a line matching up with what you are fishing for, so at least 10 lb. test at a minimum. Larger test is recommended but remember the cheaper the line the more stiff and unmanageable it gets as you get higher lb. test.

Medium Heavy and Heavy spin cast or bait cast combos. These rods will bring in the 5 lb. to over 100 lb. fish that the guys will keep coming back for on piers. Fish such as: King Mackerel, Tarpon, Cobia, Grouper in some areas, large Red and Black Drum (they can top well over 40 pounds on piers with ease), Sharks and large Skates/Stingrays.

Versions of all of these types of rods can be bought at local places like Wal-Mart, Dicks or Bass Pro at economy prices. Catfish poles are a popular item on piers. They cost about 20-30 bucks and serve you well as a medium or medium/heavy rod that you can catch most fish on a pier with. Higher end versions can certainly be bought with the sky being the limit on prices. Things like how many ball bearings, stainless steel parts and such all have bearing for the guy who will fish this stuff every week or multiple times a week, but for the occasional fisherman the cheap stuff if properly cared for, can catch you just as many fish and last many years. Simply washing off your reel and rod after each use with freshwater can lengthen its service dramatically.

Chapter 3

Tips on where and when to go

First, to really enhance your performance simply call the pier you are going to ahead of time and ask "what is biting", that little amount of effort can enable you to bring the right poles, tackle and bait. Having just one of those 3 wrong can cause you to catch nothing while everybody around you gets tired from filling their coolers with fish. I have seen it happen and you don't want to be that guy. Most all piers have either websites with 'what's biting' sections or have someone who will give you an idea of what is hitting and on what bait. After you have covered those bases, you just need to grab your poles and your friends to start the adventure.

The best fishing buddy a Dad can ever have. Only thing missing is the fisherman smell . . . somehow, she still always smells sweet!

Chapter 4

Croaker, Spot, Sea Bass and Whiting (Va. Mullet)

These fish on the coasts are very much sought after and are great fish to eat and thankfully, are very plentiful.

Equipment

Lightweight or medium tackle with a 2 hook leader rig that you can purchase at any sporting good store or Wal-Mart. (Buy 'SPOT' hooks at the pier if they have them or a long shank steel hook with about ¼" between shank and barb.) If you don't have a leader, no worries. Take a half ounce egg weight or larger if there is a lot of wave action and put it on your line then attach a barrel swivel. Now attach a piece of your fishing line (always carry a partially used fishing line spool to make homemade leaders, it is a whole lot easier to replace just the hook if the line is broken off or bitten off instead of losing your weight too) and then tie on your hook with your favorite knot.

HOOK RECOMMENDATION: EAGLE CLAW 2X LONG #6

Bait

Fresh shrimp and bloodworms work the best and you don't need much. A half inch piece of cut and peeled shrimp put on a small circle hook will entice most any of these fish. Fresh bait always outperforms but if you only have frozen shrimp, you make do. With Bloodworms you cut off about an inch or a little less and that will bring them in when nothing else will, but bloodworms can be hard to find and are expensive, so make the most out of the bites you get on them.

Cut bait of any variety: squid, small (legal to use as cut bait, check your regulations locally) fish of any type can also work in a pinch. Just keep the pieces small to increase your hook sets. Using circle hooks can help tremendously too. These hooks enable you to hook the fish in the lips/jaws instead of deeper down in the throat and also seem to simply assist with more hook sets.

Artificial baits such as: Fish bites in blood worm flavor or Gulp bloodworms can put fish on the line and some folks argue that they produce as much or more than live bait. They go on your same hooks and are fished the same way, on the bottom.

Technique: Fish on the bottom and keep your line tight. Fish anywhere from straight down by the pier pylons to as far as you can throw; just remember to pay attention to where you have thrown your last cast. Because once you find the fish and get a hit or catch one you need to cast back to that same area due to these fish are all schooling species and where there is one there is normally a ton of them. Just remember though, a school is feeding while moving and while you may tear them up for 5-30 minutes straight they can suddenly be gone. But, take note of where you were catching them because there may be some underwater depression, structure or sandbar that draws them to that area. If it draws them once it will likely draw them again.

These are things you take note of and literally write down if need be, to increase your productivity on the next trip. If you like fishing write down the date, time, weather, locations of fish and the water temp if you have it and you will be surprised at how often you can refer back to those notes and the help it will give you.

A nice catch of whiting on ice. Great fighters for their size and excellent fare.

Chapter 5

Small Bluefish, Spanish Mackerel

Equipment: Light medium to Medium spin cast combo or a typical bass fishing bait cast combo will work too.

Bait: Gotcha plugs, Diamond jigs and spoons.

Technique: You simply tie a Gotcha plug on when you have heard that the Bluefish and/or Spanish Mackerel are running. Be prepared though because the piers will be elbow to elbow with everyone fishing a plug with two mean looking treble hooks on it. But it can be an unbelievable amount of fun!

When using a Gotcha for Blues the color doesn't seem to matter so much. When they are biting they will hit anything. But, rest assured the most favored/popular out there is the white tube with the red head. It is classic 'Gotcha.' Blue heads are good too as are the shiny tube versions and even the ones with a skirt on the rear. Just bear in mind that Blues have teeth and you will be donating some to their voracious appetites, so I wouldn't spend too much on the fancy ones unless you just like the look of them for the few minutes they are resting in your tackle box.

You cast the Gotcha out as far as possible and then hold your pole over the rail of the pier with the tip down toward the water and grip the rod with your hand on the outside of the rod handle opposite of how you normally hold it. You then flick the tip of the rod outward, reel in your slack and jerk inward (toward the pier) all the while having the rod tip pointed straight at the water. This action causes a wicked reaction by the plug and the blue fish go crazy. You just keep repeating this until you make it back to the pier or hook up with a bluefish. Sometimes you will get two 1-2 lb. Bluefish on one Gotcha plug at a time because they are in such a frenzy. Don't fall in, they might work you over like a Pirahna!

Watch the guys around you too, if you aren't getting hits, speed up or slow your retrieve, give a harder or softer jerk. You just have to get in the zone with what the fish want and then just hang on cause it's crazy good fun catching Bluefish on a pier. You very well could catch a hundred 1-3 lb. fish in one exhausting day doing this. An extra tip is always to give the lure a couple bounces when you get it to the pier, let it sink then pop it back up. You can draw a lot of extra hits that way because the Bluefish are definitely patrolling the pier also. Our friend the Spanish Mackerel is usually hand in hand with the Bluefish and I encounter a large percentage of mine right at the pier when finishing my retrieve.

If you are targeting the Spanish or if they are the only thing running (no blues) the Gotcha will still work. However, a lot of time the Spanish may hit them better if you allow them to sink a bit longer prior to retrieving them. Sometimes with Spanish I don't do the rod tip down jigging, instead I throw it out, let it sink and then do a normal upright jig with a quick retrieve. Just allow it to sink down a ways after each jerk or two. Spanish like a very erratic bait and the jerk really gets their attention. They are very fast too so don't worry that they cannot catch the bait because they can. With mackerel and Blues always check your line after every catch or even after missed strikes. Look for damaged or frayed line from their teeth. If noticed, cut it off and retie and save your money instead of losing your bait!

With Spanish spoons are a great lure and they can be retrieved quickly through the water with their natural action or they can be jigged as the Gotcha plug is. With a Diamond lure you do a little more: You tie a snap swivel to your line then take a 3' section of line and 4-8 Gold hooks with spacing between the barb and shank of approximately the width of your pinky finger nail. Any type will work though most people use a crappie type long shank hook. You tie a loop at the top of the line to hook on the swivel and the drop down 6" and tie a gold hook on with a loop knot if possible (basically make a loop with the hook hanging off of it and the knot being against the line leader instead of on the hook, like a teardrop) then drop down 6 more inches and repeat until your last 6 inches and then you tie on the Diamond Jig. With this you simply throw it out and keep your line tight so it doesn't collapse on itself and tangle and then you begin to jig it. Bounce up then let it fall with tension on the line. The Spanish go crazy over this and you can catch multiple on one line. The blues will destroy this rig though, so beware if they are in a frenzy nearby. This rig is also very effective right next to a pier where you will see some folks just simply jigging this type rig up and down with a long pole on Mackerel set ups. It is effective and will catch fish on the bare hooks as much as on the jigs, (Yes, a bare hook really will catch fish ☺).

Spanish Mackerel on the hook

A small catch of Blues, often we give away over a hundred while jigging on the piers with our Gotcha plugs. Shown are a few small ones we kept to filet.

Chapter 6

Sheepshead and Spadefish

Equipment: light to medium tackle for the smaller ones, up to heavy for the big bruisers 5lb's. on up.

Bait: fiddler crabs, sand crab (mole crabs), barnacles and shrimp

HOOK RECOMMENDATION: EAGLE CLAW WIDE BEND #6 OR #8

Technique: First off it must be said that Sheepshead are a difficult fish to catch, they are relatively easy to find but can take a lot of bait before you get the 'feel' for catching them. With these steps and tips you may lessen your agony while targeting these delicious, hard fighting fish. Number one, you must know their habitat. Sheepshead have large 'sheep like' teeth, hence the name. They use these to crunch crustaceans like fiddler and mole crabs and the common barnacles you see on pylons. When they feed on these baits they crunch them with their teeth while inhaling the 'meat' and expelling the shells. So, they are not necessarily taking these baits deep into their mouth but instead nibbling on them. Therefore their bite can be light and to make things worse when you try to set the hook you may just strike the hard underside of their sheep like teeth which are hard as a rock. So, you have to use a few tricks to hook them regularly.

Let's start with the bait though. For fiddler crabs you can catch your own if you know a place where they frequent. Some bait shops sell them and that can definitely save you time. Mole crabs can be caught on the beaches as well if you know where to look and how to recognize their habitat. With shrimp, fresh is better, though about a 1-2" section peeled and cut works best when they will bite shrimp. With barnacles, simply scrape them off of a pylon into a bucket with salt water covering them and a towel over the top to keep the sun off of them if it is hot outside.

With the fiddler crab turn it on its back and you will see a flap that you can pull back with your hook tip, do so and poke your hook through that soft area that you expose and then run the hook out one of the leg holes until the barb is exposed. The mole crab is best hooked in one side and out the other. Feed the shrimp onto the hook with the barb exposed. Now with barnacles you can get creative and get some pretty good results that might shock the old timers you are competing with. Here's the trick, before you head out for the day raid the wife's collection of old pantyhose if you can get away with it, or just cut out as large of a section from a pair as you can get away with! Bring it with you and cut it into 2" squares. You will also need some small rubber bands or sewing string will work too. What you do is take an old rag and lay a small handful of the barnacles on it and then crunch them up with your heel or a hammer or similar implement. You don't have to get them into mush, per se, but just get the juices flowing from within a bit. Transfer the mutilated barnacles into the pantyhose square and then close it up around them and tie or rubber band the top shut. Now run your circle hook right through the little pouch you have made. The trick with this is that the sheepshead smells their favorite food and begins to 'crunch' it as it normally does to extract the meat from inside and this allows you to actually feel their hit. As they are trying to suck the meat out the panty hose slows them down giving you much more time than usual to set the hook. Some folks just run a hook through a barnacle or two and fish them that way but you have to almost jerk before they bite it to catch them. Now for trick number 2: With this one check your local rules on treble hook usage. As long as you can use them in your area, get the small ones that are normally around a #6. They are about a half inch wide. Now go to the dollar store or raid the leftover Halloween candy and get the cheap pink gum in the blue and yellow wrapper that everybody gives out when they are too cheap to buy real candy! There is a good use for it with Sheepshead, it can help you catch fish. Repeat the above process for smashing your barnacles while chewing a piece of the Pepto Bismol flavored gum. Now put the gum on the treble hooks covering the barbs and then roll that gum all around the busted barnacles until it is heavily coated. When the sheepshead smell that bait they run up, begin to crunch and since there are 3 hooks they literally force one or more into the meat of their jaws. Bingo, you have dinner! Sheepshead can be fished for right next to the pylons and as long as you can see barnacles on the poles there are usually fish nearby. However, if the pier isn't too crowded just walk the side until you spot the fish feeding. They are easy to see when it is sunny because they turn on their sides sometimes to pluck the barnacles off the poles. Anywhere you see one there are usually plenty more and you will likely see some monsters there if you look long enough. A final tip on fishing this way: you may encounter big Black Drum hitting these same baits presented the same way. If they are juveniles they will even look similar since they will have black stripes on their bodies too. Once over about 10 pounds they turn more silver and can be distinguished easier. These are great fish too but they do not have the tell tale buck teeth.

Spadefish hit right alongside the Sheepshead and are great fighters.

Chapter 7

Pompano

When the Pompano are running it is your chance to catch a very sought after food fish that is a fantastic fighter. Along with that, they are relatively easy to catch if you fish in the right areas.

Equipment: light to medium tackle.

HOOK RECOMMENDATION: EAGLE CLAW WIDE BEND #6 0R #8

Bait: mole crabs, shrimp and bloodworms

Technique: For Pompano you can get the occasional fellow pretty much anywhere but if you want to be the guy with the full cooler you have to fish where they are feeding. Pompano are notorious for raiding the beach in a school eating everything in their way. They are normally looking for the small mole crabs, which is one of their preferred foods. If you have some fresh live mole crabs hang on for some nice fish. If you can't get fresh ones try the frozen. If you can't get either you can use shrimp or bloodworms which will both catch nice fish though not as effectively as the mole crabs do. If no fresh bait is available at all you can use Gulp Mole Crab synthetic baits which really do work. You just have to be quick on the hook set with those because the texture is not the same as what the actual crab would be and you don't want to give them time to spit the bait out. Pompano normally feed just behind the first breaker and sometimes in the 'dirty' water in front of the breakers at a lower tide. If they are feeding in the 'dirty' water (just water that has the sand stirred up in it by the swirling tide) you simply toss your bait and allow it to sit on the bottom with a tight line. If you are fishing a single hook rig you can lightly drag it but must be careful not to drag your bait off. When fishing the backside of the breakers (toward the ocean or gulf) it is usually better to just allow the bait to sit, the water is not as turbulent and sight as well as smell will draw the fish quick enough. As with all bottom fishing be mindful where you cast. Once you hook a fish you definitely want to know where to throw when you bait back up. A tip that can increase your hookups is to use the mole crabs that may have eggs attached to their bellies first. The pompano seem to make a bee line for these and if you have a bunch of female crabs you have a lot of potential for a nice plate of fish that night.

Pompano, when they are in, can be taken by the dozens. An excellent table fish.

Chapter 8

Speckled Sea Trout

Equipment: medium tackle

HOOK RECOMMENDATION: EAGLE CLAW WIDE BEND #6 FOR CUT BAIT, IF LIVE BAIT EAGLE CLAW CIRCLE SEA 4/0

Bait: Fresh shrimp (live), Fresh shrimp (unfrozen), Live finger mullet, Spec rigs (2 buck tail jigs separated by 20 inches with a weight attached between them on a leader) and Gulp Shrimp 3 or 4 inch on a jig head commensurate with the current.

Technique: On a pier you can catch some very nice sea trout if you can present tasty and appealing bait to the picky fish.

First off, if it is not crowded and you are allowed to float fish, a live shrimp hooked behind the brain and out the back suspended 24-36"s below a bobber can be deadly on trout in calm, clear water. If the water is choppy you may have to play with the depth to get close to where the fish are suspended and feeding. In clear water they can more easily see the bait. If you don't have live you can hook a fresh dead shrimp the same as the live and as long as there is some wave action it will do a fair enough job mimicking a live shrimp. If you can catch finger mullet you place them on an 18" leader behind a barrel swivel with a 'water current' appropriate egg sinker on top. Always hook them just through the lips or through the tail and toss them out and move them ever so slowly back toward you or allow them to sit a couple minutes and then inch them toward you and allow them to sit again. If you want to keep the mullet alive you can't cast him over and over or he will die. However, a dead finger mullet can be good bait too; you just change your presentation. If he is dead you keep him rigged the same way or you can move the hook deeper into the head so it doesn't pull out and then you give sideways tugs as you work it back toward you. Hang onto the rod though because many lunkers of the sea will take this presentation, not just Speckled Sea trout. Spec rigs are made up of two buck tail walleye type jigs on a leader. Basically you have a loop that you tie onto and attached to that loop is an 8-12 inch drop line that has a buck tail jig on it then also attached to the loop is the main leader which extends about 20-24 inches with a spot midway for you to attach a tear drop weight appropriate for the current and then at the end of the leader is the second buck tail jig. Basically you cast that rig out and then slowly "jig" it back in. Raise it up, let it drop, twitch here and there. You just got to find out what the fish want that day by trial and error. A trick I use is to tip the hooks on the buck tail jigs with about a half inch piece of synthetic fish bite or Gulp bloodworm. This puts off a powerful scent that is noticed with a slow presentation. You can also tip with shrimp or squid but you run the risk of having it 'pecked' off by the bait stealing pinfish and the like. I hooked the biggest flounder I ever ran into while fishing in Fernandina Beach, Florida off of an old decommissioned bridge while using a Speck rig tipped with synthetic bloodworm. I think the locals contemplated tossing me off of the bridge after initially chuckling about the 2 foot long 'mess' I chucked over the side. I doubt anyone thought it would hook a monster on the first cast 60 feet away from the bridge. They did appreciate the fact that I wasn't going to keep the fish since I was travelling the next day, they were more than happy to 'dispose' of a nice flounder for a weary traveler ☺!

Chapter 9

Black Drum

Equipment: Medium to heavy tackle

HOOK RECOMMENDATION: SMALLERDRUM EAGLE CLAW WIDE BEND #6, LARGER DRUM-EAGLE CLAW 4/0 OR 5/0 CIRCLE SEA

Bait: cut shrimp, oysters, barnacles and blue crab (or other local crab)

Technique: Black Drum can be a fantastic fish to catch and one that rivals grouper for flavor when under 10 lbs. Over 10 lbs. many folks say the meat is too coarse. Another common complaint is that they are definitely prone to parasites, which aren't harmful if cooked, but are pretty nasty to look at when cleaning your fish. Nothing like pulling a 4 inch white worm out of a nice, fresh fillet! They get these I am told because of their prime diet of oysters. Kinda makes me rethink the idea of raw oysters after seeing the 4 inch white worm that is so common to these fish, yuck!

Fish for these with fresh shrimp near any oyster beds or structure that you can see from the pier at low tide. At night, after the Pin fish leave, you can catch black drum under the pier around the pylons. They will bite on the freshest shrimp, old stinky shrimp, GULP baits and even cut crabs. Barnacles make a great bait for them too laced inside a piece of pantyhose with a hook through the baggie.

Fishing cold weather in the tidal creeks can produce some very nice fish.

Another nice catch of cooler weather fish. Probably 70 under slot Red Drum were caught that day with only the keeper being in slot. But, the 70 plus sure made for a lot of great fishing! Author's friend Jay and his son Lucas together for the trip.

Chapter 10

Red Drum

Equipment: Medium to Heavy tackle depending on what size drum you target.

HOOK RECOMMENDATION: SMALL PUPPY DRUM-EAGLE CLAW WIDE BEND #6, LARGER DRUM, OVER SLOT FISH EAGLE CLAW CIRCLE SEA 4/0 OR 5/0.

Bait: cut or whole shrimp, oysters, crab, small up to 8" bait fish either cut or live.

Technique: First, when on a pier you need to know a general size of what Red Drum you are targeting because these guys can get huge and fight nasty. A normal keeper is by most standards 18-27 inches long and these are termed 'puppy drum' in some locales. They are called that because even though these guys may weigh close to 10 pounds they are mere pups compared to the big boys that lurk nearby.

Let's start with the pups though. For these, a nice Medium or flexible heavy rod is just right when on a pier. You will normally find these fellows pretty close in to the surf but sometimes they will be right under a pier near the pilings feeding in schools on the small minnows that take shelter there. For these you will need nothing more than cut or live shrimp when they are biting or a small piece of crab/oyster. When they are "in" they are in. Fish near the pilings and be ready to reel them in quick before they wrap around the supports. For the smaller fish you can just pull them up but the ones above 5 pounds will generally require you to use a landing net. A small mud minnow under a cork or even on the bottom will work wonders for the Red Drum as well and is a preferred food of these fish. Just remember to not use too big of a minnow or cut bait because if the puppy drum are nearby their gigantic mommies and daddies are probably close by and it gets expensive feeding those guys tackle if you aren't fishing with the right equipment.

Now with the large red Drum or 'Bull' drum you need a heavy weight rod or surf rod/reel combo. These guys can get really big and take you for a ride. I have personally had new 50# test line snapped by a red drum just beyond the last breaker. I hooked him on a trolling rod set up to catch offshore fish. I used this rod on the pier to fight the drum and the 50 # test still wasn't enough for that rare monster that loves to swallow a 4" pinfish whole! I have brought in up to 25 pound Red Drum with no issue on a pier, right above the breakers, what fun! For these guys preferred bait is a small fish up to about 8" in length. They will eat most anything but small mullet are normal bait for them. If you are allowed to use small whiting in your area these will work great as well. Hook these baits in a meaty portion about an inch forward of the tail and put them on a bottom rig with at least a foot of leader below your weight, then toss them next to pilings or just oceanside of the last breaker. If there are any Red Drum in the area, and those are their preferred feeding areas, they will grab that fish in a heartbeat. If I am fishing two rods and they are biting I generally don't even have time to throw out number two because they will hit so fast.

Another trick for Red Drum is to throw your bait with a nice steel leader of say 18" under the pier. This is a favorite haunt of the big reds and more often than not you will get a monster soon after.

Don't be surprised when fishing for Red Drum during the late summer/fall if you hook a nice striper/rockfish instead. This species can hardly resist the same meal you present for the Reds.

When you get on the Red Drum you can really be ON the Reds. These fish sometimes have a blue sheen to them when they are feeding really well. It makes them even more beautiful.

Chapter 11

Flounder

Equipment: Medium weight rod

HOOK RECOMMENDATION: EAGLE CLAW CIRCLE SEA 3/0

Bait: Live mud or mullet minnow preferably or a small pinfish with the dorsal fin trimmed off with a pair of shears.

Technique:

Fish for the Flounder with an egg sinker above a barrel swivel tied off to a 12-24" monofilament leader. Use a good circle hook and hook the minnow 2-4" long either through the lips or just above the tail in the meaty part (take care not sever the spine or hit the brain when hooking either end). You will drop this bait right next to pilings which are the preferred ambush points for pier dwelling flounder. Let the bait set and give the flounder about 15-30 minutes to take the bait before moving to another piling. Some folks fish each piling with this rig only stopping for a minute or two at each one. This will work if you drop it very close to the fish as long as you don't scare it off. But, 30 minutes at each one will give the skittish fish more opportunity to be fooled and wind up on your hook. Just be mindful that if Red Drum, Stripers or Cobia are nearby you may wind up with a fantastic fight as an added bonus!

Here is a nice catch of coastal Flounders with a slot Drum thrown in to boot. Not bad for a few hours of fun in Paradise!

Chapter 12

Inshore Fishing

Inshore fishing for the weekend angler can be tiring, expensive and, unfortunately, less than rewarding sometimes. However, there are ways to make your trip into something that will keep you coming back. Though you may not limit out on your first trip, you can certainly gain valuable experience and still put some fish in the boat.

First, set reasonable expectations. Don't get upset if you don't catch the quality or quantity of fish like you see the professionals on television bring in. Remember, they have often times paid for advice, fished the area for days and enlisted the help of guides for pre-fishing prior to the taping of the show. They also have access to unlimited tackle and bait. You, on the other hand, have to make do with the tackle you have and with what bait is available at a price that is affordable to you.

Next, target a fish that is always there and always hangs around the same structure. Obviously, things like storms (barometer changes, tides etc.) all come into play but there are some saltwater fish who are creatures of habit and you can take advantage of their routine. Begin by looking around the area you will be fishing via sites like Google Maps or one of the many others. Put in the address of your ramp where you will launch and then expand out to the areas you likely will fish. Look for the obvious things like bridges, old pilings or docks. All of these areas are visible through a satellite image and all will hold types of fish. These Fish can be fighters, are generally plentiful and great to eat!

Chapter 13

Inshore Black Drum

HOOK RECOMMENDATION: EAGLE CLAW WIDE BEND #6

Equipment: Medium weight rod

Bait: cut shrimp, mole crab (sand fleas), cut crab and oysters

Technique: Fish near oyster beds where you see 'noodling' evidence left by black drum. Basically, round holes in the sand where they have rooted around eating crustaceans. Fish near deep holes in tidal creeks, especially in colder weather. These fish will stay put and will be drawn to a deep, warm pocket of water until the shallow water warms back up. They will eat anything then. Fish near buoys or pilings where there are deep depressions. These fish frequent these spots to feed around.

Place your bait on a circle hook attached to a fluorocarbon leader of less than 12" attached to a barrel swivel with a half to two ounce egg sinker above it. Literally drop the bait right into the target area and be prepared for a light bite up to a strong 'drag away" action. Once hooked these fish usually fight downward and just pull away from you instead of swimming side to side or all over. They have their own style of resistance to being pulled in.

Chapter 14

Inshore Red Drum

Equipment: Light to medium Spinning tackle or easy casting bait caster.

HOOK RECOMMENDATION: CUT BAIT-EAGLE CLAW WIDE BEND #6, LIVE BAIT-EAGLE CLAW CIRCLE SEA 3/0, 4/0 OR 5/0

Bait: Live or cut shrimp, Oysters, Cut fish, Mud minnows, mullet minnows and artificial baits.

Technique: Look for feeding schools when the water is calm enough to see them. Look for skipping baitfish or large swirls of adult fish pushing bait up into the creeks. When you see them, toss your natural cut or live bait on a 12" or less Flourocarbon leader in front of the school and hang on for a fish. If they are feeding you can catch quality fish for hours off of one school. Just be quiet and try not to spook them. If you are fishing artificial use a Gulp or Mirrolure presentation if you are just starting out. A 3" Gulp artificial shrimp in 'new penny" scheme on a wide set jig head of ¼ or 3/8 ounce can be deadly. Throw this right in front or inside of feeding schools and gently work it according to how a real shrimp moves. There are plenty of you tube videos of how to fish Gulp shrimp. The Reds love these baits. A Mirrolure top water is deadly too when the water is calm, the reds will tear it up so hang on. Favorite haunts for these fish are oyster beds and tidal creeks. Look for them in shallows pushing baits.

Now, if it's hot out or the Reds are being real finicky you may have to splurge on some live mud minnows/mullet minnows or catch your own with a cast net. Use a nice sized foam bobber of about 2-4 inches and place your 2-4 inch minnow with 1-2 foot of Flourocarbon leader beneath the cork. Throw this presentation into small tidal pools, cuts and creeks where you see Reds feeding or fish blindly along the edge of saw grass and oyster bars. If there are fish around they have a hard time passing up these treats!

Chapter 15

Inshore Speckled Sea Trout

Equipment: Light to medium tackle

HOOK RECOMMENDATION: EAGLE CLAW CIRCLE SEA 3/0

Bait: Live shrimp or artificial baits

Technique: Fish the tidal creeks off of bays, rivers, or intercoastal waterway. These trout will be around and can go pretty far inland to creeks as long as there is enough salinity for them to function and there is not a cold shock which sometimes stuns them causing large fish kills. Fish a 3-4" Gulp shrimp on a wide mouth jig head slowly along the bottom near structure and deep holes. If trout are near they will hit the Gulp hands down to most bait. You can refreshen it from time to time with Gulp spray or a re-dunk in the container. It is common to catch 40 plus trout on 1 Gulp shrimp with ease. Mirro-lures work well also for the trout and will outperform the Gulp on occasion. They require some talent to fish and can be expensive when lost over the plastics. If the bite is slow you can use live shrimp under a cork along the creek edges, up into cuts or along structure. The trout find this hard to resist and often will leave you wishing you had brought just "one more' dozen shrimp!

Chapter 16

Inshore Flounder

Equipment: Light to medium tackle

HOOK RECOMMENDATION: EAGLE CLAW CIRCLE SEA 3/0 OR 4/0

Bait: Live shrimp, mud minnows, live mullet or artificial baits

Techniques: Fish any slow or still water that is right off of rapidly flowing water. The flounder is an ambush predator and a smart one at that. They anchor down where there is little resistance but where they expect to catch disabled or physically spent bait to come by. Bait that is traveling in the fast running water can make an easy meal for a foraging flounder. The flounder is a much sought after fish and one that can put up a heck of a fight.

If using live bait place an egg shaped sinker 1–3 ounce dependent upon bait size and current and tie a swivel beneath it. Then place your circle hook on a leader 18-24" beneath it with the bait hooked your favorite way. I prefer to hook through the lips if I will be moving the bait occasionally but through the lower pectoral fin if allowing it to sit stationary as when fishing multiple poles. The swivel and leader beneath the weight will allow the bait to swim freely and also let the flounder pull the bait out gently letting it consume it completely, allowing for good hook sets.

When fishing artificial you can buy many items marketed for flounder. Myself, I still stick with the good 'old Gulp shrimp or mullet minnow. Fish these low and slow and wait for that familiar bump before you get your flattie. Fish enough ground and feel enough 'bumps' and you will become one of the 'flounder finders' and make yourself proud and your table full. There's lots of these fish out there and they are very tasty to boot!

Now Guys and Gals this first edition will have hopefully turned you on to the ability to fish and CATCH without quickly losing interest. The more of us who fish the longer we will be able to keep passing this wondrous past time on to our kids.

Most any fisherman has techniques that fill their coolers and they are hard pressed to turn loose of those secrets. I respect that, but we have to be willing to help the novice fisherman out or when we are all gone there won't be anyone to lobby for fishermen's rights for our kids. As long as there are good catch/keep ratios and bountiful clean water, our past time will continue.

In my next issue I will give you some tips for how to use freshwater techniques with astounding success when in salt! I also will tell you how to start combining baits to make your line be the one that gets hit when no one else's does.

Coming soon, a freshwater how to manual like our saltwater one above will be available. It just takes me time to stay out of the water long enough to let my ink dry!

Until then, be friends to our fish so we can fish with our friends !!!!!!!!!!!!!!!!!!!!!!!!!!!!!!!

Brian P 10/01/11

Made in the USA
San Bernardino, CA
01 March 2020